You Know Better Than That

by
Norah Smaridge

Drawings by Susan Perl

Abingdon Press
Nashville and New York

Library of Congress Cataloging in Publication Data

Smaridge, Norah. You know better than that.
SUMMARY: Fourteen humorous verses advise
on correct conduct. [1. Etiquette—Poetry] I. Perl,
Susan, illus. II. Title.
PZ8.3.S637Ym   395'.1'22   72-7033
ISBN 0-687-467446

FOR
❀Rochelle Rubin
with love and thanks
for her helpful advice

At home you sometimes do things, which
You know you SHOULDN'T do
(Like jumping stairs, or kicking chairs,
Or leaving all your stew).
Then Mother scolds, or maybe spanks,
Or even tells your Dad,
For when you misbehave at home
That's really very bad!

It's just as bad, or even worse,
To make yourself a pest
At Gran's, or Joan's, or Peter's,
Or wherever you're a guest.
So here (in case you should forget)
Are poems, just for you,
That tell about the kind of thing
A guest should NEVER do.

ARE YOU LISTENING, DEAR?

Whenever you are asked to come
And play at Peter Gray's,
Please pay attention carefully
To what his mother says.

And if she says, "Don't use the swing,
It's time it had a check,"
Then keep away—unless you'd like
To break your little neck.

And when she warns, "Don't jump those steps!"
You'd really better not.
You might fall flat and bump your nose,
The only one you've got.

She doesn't like to spoil your fun,
She doesn't mean to fuss,
But in HER house and in HER yard
She knows what's DANGEROUS.

She only wants to send you home
With all of you complete,
And NOT with missing teeth in front
And band-aids on your seat.

HOLD YOUR HORSES!

When you're in someone else's house
Why must you always RUN?
Why not slow down when people frown
And WALK, like everyone?

You run, run, run, around the rooms
And up and down the stairs,
Until your hostess wrings her hands
And starts to say her prayers.

A nonstop train? A bus? A plane?
A high-speed racing car?
A kangaroo on roller skates?—
What DO you think you are?

When you're at home, you're not allowed
To run like crazy, dear
(Unless the house has caught on fire),
So PLEASE don't do it here.

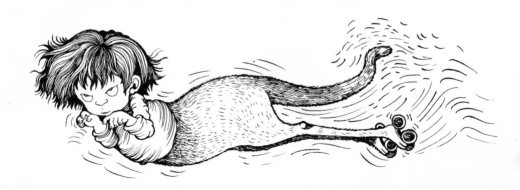

YOU KNOW HOW IT IS

When visiting, you'll always find
It's best to leave your pet behind.
Some folks have things called AL-LER-GIES
And dogs and rabbits make them SNEEZE.

Some kids are sure to quake and shake
If you should bring your garter snake
(Even a spider gives them shocks
Although you keep him in a box).

Oh, never, never take your mouse
To play in someone else's house,
For if he makes the tiniest squeak
Ladies are going to jump and shriek.

Besides, that house might have a CAT—
And that would be the end of THAT.

HANG UP!

The telephone, no matter where,
Is NOT a toy for YOU.
It's fun to dial—but just suppose
You reach KAL-A-MA-ZOO!

That call would cost an awful lot,
And oh, we'd hate to say,
Just what will happen, dear, to you
When Daddy has to pay.

LOCKED IN

Unless you're certain as can be
That it will open EASILY,
In someone else's house, be sure
You never lock the bathroom door.
You might get stuck, and then the fuss
Would really be PRE-POS-TER-OUS.

People would bang the door and shout
And wonder how to get you out
(The window would be much too high
Unless, of course, you've learned to fly).

You'd have to wait while someone ran
To find a handy handyman,
And think of the EX-AS-PER-ATION
If he has left for his vacation!

No one could wash or take a shower
For there you'd sit, hour after hour,
With just the bath stool for a seat
And nothing but some soap to eat.

JUST WASH YOUR HANDS

At Jane's, when you have played with glue,
Or any kind of guck or goo,
Or rocks, or earth, or mud instead,
Or p'raps a frog, extremely dead,
OF COURSE your hostess understands
You need to go and wash your hands.

But that is ALL you need to do—
You need not spray the ceiling, too,
Or wash the window, soap the door,
Or slop some water on the floor,
Or wad the towel in a ball—
Jane's mother won't like THAT at all!

And if you leave her pink soap BLACK
She's never going to ask you back.

FAIR'S FAIR

At Bob's, at home, and everywhere,
Remember you're supposed to SHARE.
Divide the crayons into two,
That's half for Bob, and half for you,
Divide the jigsaw bits in three,
For Jennifer, and you, and Lee,
Divide the box of modeling stuff,
So everybody has enough.

(Of course you can't divide the cat—
Don't try to be as fair as THAT!)

FLOOD WARNING

When you have poured yourself a drink
At Mrs. Johnson's kitchen sink,
Please TURN THE FAUCET OFF, before

You fill the sink

And flood the floor

And flood the room

And flood the hall

And flood the yard

And road and all.

The house would start to sail away,
THEN what would Mrs. Johnson say?
Her home would be a floating ark—
And THAT's a tricky thing to park.

OUT OF PLACE

You know what happens when you leave
Your blocks on Daddy's chair.
(He jumps sky-high, and wants to know
What they are DOING there!)

The playroom is where toys belong
As you have surely found—
So, when you play in someone's house,
Don't leave his toys around.

The kitchen floor is NOT the place
Where puzzles should be spread,
And trucks and trains do NOT belong
On Mrs. Brewer's bed.

And, on her pretty pink settee,
She won't be pleased to find
A pastepot and a sticky brush,
Which YOU have left behind.

And NEVER leave a baseball
On the stairs at Mrs. Jones'—
If someone trips, YOU'LL be to blame
For all his broken bones!

KEEP OUT!

When visiting in Peter's house
It's rude as rude can be
To open drawers, and peek inside
To see what you can see.

They're only full of shirts and shorts
And socks, and stuff like that
(Except the drawer in Peter's room—
It's full of Peter's cat).

It's not polite to open the
Refrigerator door—
Haven't you seen some margarine
And cheese and stuff before?

It's rude to look in closets, too,
Mother has OFTEN said—
Besides, a box might tumble down
And crack you on the head!

NOW, BEFORE YOU GO HOME...

You tidy up your room at home
(It only takes a minute,
Except when you've been cutting things
Or eating popcorn in it).

So, when you've played in Susan's house,
Please do a nice big cleanup,
Put toys away, and modeling clay,
And pick that jelly bean up.

Wipe off the paste from Susan's chair
Or else she's going to stick,
And take those crayons from the pup
Before they make him sick.

Then dump the junk and paper, and
That cherry soda can—
Surely you know that Susan's Mom
Is NOT a garbage man?

WHERE DID YOU GET *THAT?*

It's lots of fun, of course, to go
To Harold's house, to play
With Harold's toys—but, when you leave,
DON'T carry them away!

However much you long to keep
That model racing car,
Or need that little ping-pong ball,
You know how mothers are!

And, though it's late for supper
And you're hungry, tired, and black,
Your mother will be mad at you
And make you take it back.

So don't do what you SHOULDN'T do
When visiting and such—
Then everyone will smile "Come in!"
And like you very much.
You'll never get on people's nerves,
You'll never drive them wild,
And nobody will EVER groan,
"Here comes that AWFUL child!"

You Know Better Than That